D1220943

ON THE MAP

EGYPT

Titles in this Series:

Canada	Japan
China	Mexico
Egypt	Russia
France	Spain
Germany	U.S.A.
Italy	West Indies

Editor: Marian L. Edwards
Design: M&M partnership
Electronic production: Scott Melcer
Photographs: ZEFA except
  Robert Harding (14bl, 17br), Chris Fairclough (17tr, 19b),
  Spectrum (23r)
Map artwork: Raymond Turvey
Cover photo: Pyramids at Giza

Library of Congress Cataloging-in-Publication Data

Flint, David, 1946–
    Egypt / David Flint
      p.   cm. — (On the map)
    Includes bibliographical references and index.
    Summary: Introduces, in brief text and illustrations, the
  geography, history, culture, industries, famous landmarks,
  and people of Egypt.
    ISBN 0–8114–3420–6
    I. Title.   II. Series.
  DT49.F55 1994
  954.91–dc20   93–10995
                                                                             CIP
                                                                              AC
Printed and bound in the United States.
1 2 3 4 5 6 7 8 9 0 VH 98 97 96 95 94 93

EGYPT

David Flint

RSVP
RAINTREE
STECK-VAUGHN
PUBLISHERS
The Steck-Vaughn Company

Austin, Texas

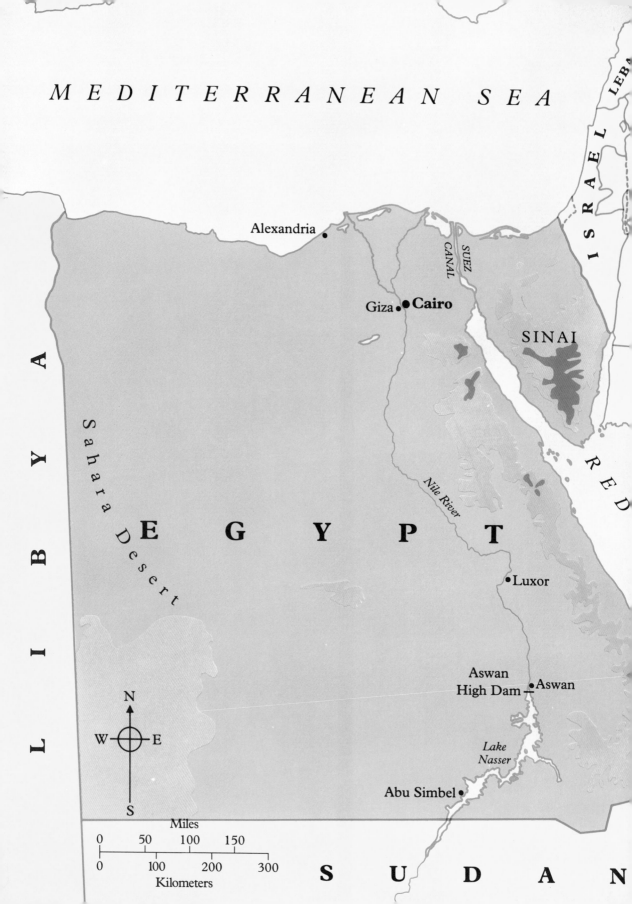

Contents

Between Africa and Europe

Egypt is a country in the northeast corner of Africa. It is connected to both the Middle East and Europe. Egypt is joined to Israel in the east, Sudan in the south, and Libya in the west. The Mediterranean Sea forms the border on the north and the Red Sea on the southeast.

The weather all over Egypt is mostly hot and dry. The country does have a cool season. In the north it is cool from December to February. Then from April to December rising temperatures reach over 100 degrees in the shade. The cool season in the south is from October to April. Summer begins in May, making the south even hotter than the north.

Over two-thirds of Egypt is desert. It has long periods of time when there is very little rain. Several years may pass between showers. In the spring, a hot, dry wind called khamsin blows across the north. It blows for fifty days, from late March through May. Blinding sandstorms are frequent, making travel in the desert very dangerous.

The warm, dry climate makes Egypt a popular place to visit year-round. No matter how hot it may have been during the day, the evenings are usually cool and pleasant.

amels are very important animals in
gypt. They can travel in the desert
r long periods without water.

Egypt has very little rain. Most of the
land is desert with hardly any grass
or trees.

Iot all of Egypt is flat. Sinai in the
ortheast has steep, rugged mountains.

For hundreds of years, fishing boats like
these have sailed the Mediterranean Sea.

Modern passenger boats take tourists to see the monuments of ancient Egypt.

Traditional boats, called feluccas, carry people and goods on the Nile.

The Aswan High Dam was built across the Nile in 1970 forming Lake Nasser.

At Aswan, new hotels serve tourists visiting Lake Nasser and the dam.

The Gift of the Nile

The Nile River is the longest river in the world. It is 4,145 miles long. The river has two parts—the White Nile and the Blue Nile. The White Nile flows out of Lake Victoria in Uganda. It joins the Blue Nile in Khartoum, Sudan. Together they enter Egypt at Lake Nasser and flow to the Mediterranean Sea.

Without the Nile River, Egypt would be entirely desert. The river has supported the people of Egypt for thousands of years. In July and August each year, floods left rich soil and silt on the nearby fields. Farmers would only plant crops they could harvest before the next floods came. Then in 1970, the Aswan High Dam was completed. It changed the yearly floods into a steady water supply for farmers.

The Aswan High Dam is more than 2 miles wide and 365 feet high. It took ten years to build. The dam stores water in Lake Nasser, which is 300 miles long.

This dam greatly improved the lives of people living along the Nile River. With the dam and Lake Nasser, the flow of water in the Nile can be controlled. People can grow more rice and cotton. Now there is plenty of water for irrigating the land. There is also a reserve for years when it does not rain. The dam brought much needed electric power to the region.

Sand Dunes and Oases

The land surface changes a lot in Egypt. In some places there are long lines of sand dunes. The sand dunes are formed by strong, hot winds sweeping through the desert. The sand often piles into dunes almost 500 feet high. In other places, the desert surface is bare rock or pebbles. Very few plants grow in these dry areas.

Although much of the desert is dry, water can be found in some places. Here and there water comes to the surface. It comes from underground wells or rivers. Date palms grow well, and farmers can plant fruits and vegetables. These places in the desert are called oases. Sometimes an oasis is only a cluster of palms around a well. A large oasis may have a grove of palm trees, gardens, and include a village or small town.

Date palms are the main trees found in an oasis. They provide a nutritious fruit, as well as cool shade from the hot sun. Branches from the date palms are used for thatching roofs on the houses.

Camel trains or caravans still carry goods across the desert. They travel from one oasis to another. An oasis is a center for trade. People who live in the desert come to buy food and other goods.

ines of sand dunes are found just a few miles from the Nile. Sand dunes are always
changing shape because the wind blows the sand along.

he Al Fayyum oasis is one of the places in the desert where water springs to the
urface. Tribes like the Bedouin spend their lives traveling from one oasis to another.

Cairo

Cairo is the capital of Egypt and the largest city in Africa. It is the center for the Egyptian government and for business and industry.

Cairo is built on both banks of the Nile River. The islands in the river are part of the city. Bridges connect them to the city. Cairo is a mixture of the very old and the new. Modern skyscrapers stand next to ancient museums and mosques. Some of the mosques are hundreds of years old. There are broad avenues and narrow, winding streets.

The streets of Cairo are often crowded with cars, buses, and trucks. This causes traffic jams and makes travel around the city very slow. The new subway has reduced some of the traffic.

About 10 million people live in Cairo. More people arrive from the countryside at the rate of a thousand a week. They come to find work in the shops and factories. Because of Cairo's housing shortage, many cannot find a place to live. As many as eight or nine people sometimes share one or two rooms.

Cairo is a popular city for tourists. Thousands visit the city each year. They come to see the mosques, museums, pyramids, and other places of interest.

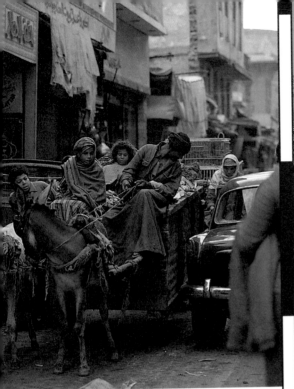

In the older parts of Cairo, the streets are very narrow. People travel around in both donkey carts and modern cars.

Tahrir Square is the center of modern Cairo. Here there are large newly built stores and hotels.

Cairo is built on both banks of the Nile River. Large modern bridges have been built to link the two parts of the city.

The Sultan Hassan Mosque. People are called to daily prayers from the tall, thin towers that are called minarets.

In some parts of the countryside, women still use the Nile for washing clothes and dishes.

For both men and women marriage is the most important event in their lives.

Apartments in Cairo. Windows are small, and shutters keep the rooms c

Family Life

In the countryside, people still follow the old ways of living. Daily life is centered on family members and growing enough food to eat. Men rise early and spend the day working in the fields and tending the animals. Women spend a great deal of time with their husbands in the fields. In addition, women cook, clean, and care for the children. They also care for older family members who are usually living with them. Children carry water to the fields and help to take care of the animals.

To relax, villagers love to celebrate. An entire village will turn out for a wedding or childbirth. It is a reason to have a big feast and to enjoy the company of others.

Family life in an Egyptian city is much different from outside the city. Women do many of the same jobs as men. They work in offices and factories. They are doctors, teacher, and engineers. Like many countries, Egypt's large cities are overcrowded and do not have enough housing. Many people are squeezed into small apartments.

Cities provide a variety of things for families to do. There are museums, libraries, theaters, and many more things to enjoy.

Food

Egyptians usually eat a light breakfast. It is often just mint tea or coffee with bread. Children drink tea or milk. The people eat large amounts of bread or aiysh. Flat, round loaves of bread are eaten with every meal.

Lunch is the main meal of the day. It is eaten between 1 and 3 o'clock in the afternoon. Lamb or pigeon dishes might be served, along with rice and salad. This is followed by fruit and cheese. Egyptians eat a variety of fruits and melons. Oranges, grapes, and lemons grow well in the rich soil. They are plentiful all year long. Chicken and rabbit, shrimp and other seafood are popular.

A light supper is eaten in the evening between 10 P.M. and 12 midnight. It might include vegetable patties with tomato salad, olives, and bread. Most farm families enjoy a hot, rich vegetable stew and bread in the evening.

The national dish of Egypt is called fool. It is made of crushed bean seeds, oil, salt, and lemon juice cooked into a thick sauce. Sometimes tomatoes are added. Fool is rich in protein and is often eaten as a mid-morning snack. When eaten for breakfast, it is served with a fried egg on top.

Fruits and vegetables fresh from the countryside arrive in the city stores each morning.

n street markets people can buy a wide ange of fresh food. They can also buy ea drawn from the samovar or urn.

A man eats a meal at an outdoor food stand. A variety of hot and cold foods can be bought.

Going to School

In Egypt all children between the ages of six and twelve must go to school. Most go to kindergarten from age four until they are six. Then they go to elementary school until they are twelve years old. From age twelve to fifteen, students can attend a school that prepares them for high school. English and French are taught in this school. The government pays for all elementary and high school education. Students also receive a free noon meal.

In rural areas along the Nile River, many village schools hold classes outside. Children's desks are placed under trees. Many of these children leave school early to help their parents in the fields.

High school is for three years. Here students can choose the kind of training that suits their ability. There are skills centers for training in industry, agriculture, or commerce. Students planning to attend college might pick a high school for science and math. Still others enroll in art school.

After finishing high school, a student can attend a college or university. Most offer four-year courses. Egypt's universities attract students from all over Africa, Asia, and the Middle East.

gypt has a very long and important history. School children regularly
sit ancient temples, like this one at Thebes, to learn about their past.

arents know that education is very important in Egypt. They want their
hildren to do well in school and get a good job.

The Suez Canal links the Red Sea with the Mediterranean Sea, providing ships with a shorter route to Europe from Asia.

Long distance travel in Egypt is usually by train. Often people sit on the roof or stand in the doorways.

Traffic jams are a regular part of l cities and towns as more and more people own cars.

Getting Around

The Nile is an important part of all transportation in Egypt. Boats of many sizes, from feluccas and dhows to big cargo ships, use the Nile. Special paddle steamers carry tourists along the river to the ancient temples at Luxor.

Modern bridges and highways connect many towns and cities. Cairo and Alexandria are linked by two major highways. A network of trains connects Cairo with other cities. Trains run from Alexandria in the north, through the Suez Canal and Cairo, and on to Aswan in the south. The Suez Canal is a shortcut between the Mediterranean and the Red Sea. Travel by train in Egypt is comfortable and cheap. To get from place to place fast, Egypt's airlines operate between the major cities.

Few people own private cars. A car costs a lot of money, and only rich people can afford one. To get around towns and cities, people use buses, bicycles, motorcycles, donkeys, and carts. Cairo's subway system has helped to speed up travel around the city.

In desert areas, animals are the main way to get around. The donkey is the most common animal, followed by the camel. Both carry large loads over long distances. It is not unusual to see a caravan of animals slowly walking across miles of desert.

Sports and Leisure

The people of Egypt enjoy many kinds of sports. Soccer is the most popular team sport. Soccer matches are held in sports stadiums and shown on television. Young people can be seen playing soccer in any area of open space.

Egypt's climate makes it ideal for playing many kinds of sports. Sports like tennis, golf, and squash can be played year-round. Water sports are also enjoyed by many people. Most cities have swimming pools, and swimming is becoming more common. So are sailing, fishing, and waterskiing.

In schools, sports and games play an important role in children's education. Boys and girls take part in scouts and other youth groups.

Egyptians love to celebrate. Holidays and festivals bring families and friends together. Religious holidays are the high points for many families. After fasting, the people celebrate with delicious food and pastries. Families that can afford it cook big feasts and hold an open house.

Socializing with others is what Egyptians like best. After work, men meet in cafes and play backgammon, a game that is thousands of years old.

olk dancing is popular with people of l ages in Egypt. Traditional costumes re an important part of the dances.

Egyptian men enjoy the speed and competition of horse racing. Races take place in the desert.

On the Land

More than half of Egypt's people make a living off the land. They farm small plots of land near the Nile and Suez Canal. These farmers are called fellahin, and most are very poor. They raise only enough food to feed their family. Many farm families are very large. Their homes often have only two or three rooms. One of the rooms is for the farm animals.

In places where the soil is rich, the farmers do not have modern farm equipment. They still use animals to pull wooden plows. Their simple tools were developed hundreds of years ago. There is modern farm equipment for sale, but only the rich farmers can afford to buy it.

Farmers depend on water from the Aswan High Dam or from deep local wells to water their crops. They pump the water by hand to the land. Corn is the most important food crop. Many farmers also grow cotton, which has been grown since ancient times. Egypt is one of the world's leading cotton producers. Much of the cotton is exported to other parts of the world.

Although life is hard for Egypt's farmers, family ties are strong. Whole families, including aunts, uncles, and grandparents, live together. They farm small plots of land, harvesting three or four crops a year.

arvesting dates can be dangerous work. The clusters of fruit are cut down
the fall, and the whole family helps in the sorting and packing.

ew tractors work quickly and efficiently but are very expensive.
xen are cheaper but much slower.

Egyptian women work many hours
weaving beautiful, artistic pattern

Many Egyptians work in high-rise
offices, stores, markets, or in the
tourist industry.

Because many families are poor,
children work wherever they can
to earn money.

Work

Cities in Egypt offer a variety of jobs for the people. Two out of every ten people work in factories, and another two work in offices, shops, or hotels. Most large factories are in cities like Alexandria and Cairo. Workers make television sets, cars, tractors, steel, and chemicals. Other factories in or near Cairo produce textiles, paper, and sugar.

Tourism is one of the fastest growing industries. Large numbers of people from around the world visit Egypt every year. Because of this, many Egyptians have found jobs in hotels, restaurants, and as guides.

Today many Egyptians are finding work in service industries. They work in government, trade, and banking. Egyptians also find jobs in education, transportation, and information sharing.

Many people have age-old trades. That is, they work at the same jobs as their parents before them. Many are craftspeople who make jewelry, woodwork, and leather goods. They also work with metals like copper and brass. Women and children are taught to weave beautiful rugs and wall hangings.

Each morning fishers leave their villages. They sail out to catch fish in the Mediterranean and Red seas.

Famous Landmarks

The 600-foot high Cairo Tower is a modern landmark in an ancient city.

Hieroglyphics carved on temple wa tell stories of ancient Egypt.

Built 3,000 years ago as a tribute to Ramses II, in 1968 the figures at Abu Simbel were moved 200 feet up the hill to save them from the rising waters of Lake Nasser.

e Mohammed Ali Mosque, Cairo,
ilt in Turkish style in 19th century.

The Great Sphinx at Giza is carved out
of limestone and is 4,500 years old.

e monument to President Nasser built
side the Aswan High Dam on the Nile.

The death mask of Tutankhamen
discovered in his tomb in 1922.

Facts and Figures

Egypt—the Land and People

Population:	about 55 million
Area:	about 387,000 square mi
Length: (north-south)	675 mi
Width: (east-west)	770 mi
Capital city: population:	Cairo about 10 million
Language:	Arabic
Religion:	Islam but others are practiced
Money:	Egyptian pound £E1=100 piasters £E1=$.30 U.S.

Important Dates in Egyptian History

2680-2258 BC	Pharaoh dynasties rule Egypt Great Pyramid at Giza built
1405-1370 BC	Temple at Luxor built
1298-1232 BC	Ramses II builds statues at Abu Simbel
51 BC	Cleopatra becomes Queen of Egypt
30 BC	Egypt part of the Roman Empire
639-642	Muslim Arab armies conquer Egypt
1517	Egypt occupied by Turkey
1798	France occupies Egypt
1869	Suez Canal opened
1953	Egypt becomes a republic
1958	Egypt and Syria combine to form the United Arab Republic
1970	Aswan High Dam completed
1971	Name changed to Arab Republic of Egypt

Average Temperatures in Fahrenheit

	January	June
Alexandria (north)	59°F	83°F
Aswan (south)	66°F	95°F

The Hieroglyphic Alphabet

a   i-j   â   ou   b   p   f   m   n   r   h   h

kh   h   s   s'   ch   q   k   g   t   th   d   dj

Further Reading

Bennet, Olivia. *A Family in Egypt*. Lerner, 1985

Caselli, Giovanni, *The Everyday Life of an Egyptian Craftsman*.
    P. Bedrick, 1991

Department of Geography, Lerner Publications. *Egypt in Pictures*.
    Lerner, 1988

Diamond, Arthur. *Egypt: Gift of the Nile*. Macmillan Children's Book
    Group, 1992

Jacobsen, Karen. *Egypt*. Childrens, 1990

Kerr, James. *Egyptian Farmers*. Franklin Watts, 1991

Steel, Anne. *Egyptian Pyramids*. Franklin Watts, 1990

Stewart, Gail B. *Egypt*. Macmillan Children's Book Group, 1992

Index